Classic

MEXICAN

Classic

MEXICAN

Hot and spicy recipes from all over Mexico

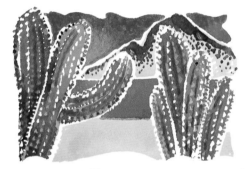

ELISABETH LAMBERT ORTIZ

SMITHMARK

This edition published in 1997 by
SMITHMARK Publishers, a division of US Media Holdings, Inc.
16 East 32nd Street
New York, New York 10016

SMITHMARK books are available for bulk purchase for sales promotion and for
premium use. For details write or call the manager of special sales,
SMITHMARK Publishers, 16 East 32nd Street,
New York, New York 10016; (212) 532-6600.

Produced by Anness Publishing Limited
Hermes House
88-89 Blackfriars Road
London SE1 8HA

ISBN 0 7651 9570 4

Publisher: Joanna Lorenz
Senior Food Editor: Linda Fraser
Project Editor: Zoe Antoniou
Designer: Annie Moss
Mac Artist: John Fowler
Photographer: David Jordan
Food Stylist: Judy Williams,
assisted by Manisha Kanani
Illustrator: Madeleine David
Jacket photographer: Thomas Odulate

Printed and bound in Singapore

Picture on frontispiece (clockwise from top left): Salsa, Tortilla Flutes, Corn Tortillas,
Tacos and Flour Tortillas.

1 3 5 7 9 10 8 6 4 2

CONTENTS

INTRODUCTION

Many of the foods we take for granted in the United States were unknown before Christopher Columbus reached the Americas in 1492. We had no corn, tomatoes or peppers (sweet, pungent or hot); no common beans such as red kidney or pinto; no pumpkins or other winter squashes. Zucchini and *chayotes* were equally unfamiliar, as were avocados and guavas, and we had never tasted chocolate or vanilla. Even turkeys were unknown. All these foods originated in Mexico where agriculture is believed to have been practiced as long ago as 7000 BC, about the same time, give or take a century or two, that the cultivation of food crops began in the Middle East. After the Conquest of Mexico by Hernando Cortés in 1521,

the Spanish introduced wheat and domesticated animals, previously unknown as food options in the Americas. Cattle yielded beef, milk, butter, cream and cheese. The domestic pig, as it was better to eat, soon ousted the local wild and wily boar; lambs, goats and the domestic hen made their appearances. The Spanish planted olive trees for olive oil, and walnut trees, as well as the vegetables that reminded them of home.

It was out of this meeting of Old and New Worlds that the cuisine of Mexico developed. This colonial kitchen still rests firmly on its Aztec and Mayan foundations, and though Mexican food is unique in the world of cooking, it is neither difficult to prepare nor inaccessible. There are no difficult or complicated techniques to master, and the unique flavors of Mexican dishes appeal to nearly everyone (and you don't have to love chili in everything!).

Many famous and popular recipes make use of the

This page: The rich and varied terrain of Mexico provides a diverse harvest of produce. Next page (clockwise from top left): avocados, string of garlic, chayote, garlic bulb, tomatoes, onions, tomatillos, canned jalapeño chilies, zucchini, lemon and lime halves.

various types of unleavened flat pancakes made from corn flour, which the Spanish called *tortillas*. This bread has the distinction of being made from cooked flour. Dried corn kernels are cooked in water with lime until they're soft and the skins can be rubbed off. The corn is then drained and ground into a heavy paste. The dried version is called *masa harina*, literally "dough flour." Although many Mexican women still make tortillas at home, some using the ancient skill of patting them out by hand, they can also be purchased uncooked or freshly-baked from *tortillerias*. Tortillas are also exported; you can now buy them packaged in most supermarkets. They are used as the basis of a number of dishes that the Spanish call *Antojitos*. These are more than just snack foods or appetizers and form a whole category in the Mexican kitchen.

Of equal importance in Mexican cooking is the family of cultivated capsicums that the Aztecs collectively called chili, although we tend to differentiate between chilies and the mild red, yellow and green bell peppers. It is estimated that there may be over a hundred varieties of chilies, sold fresh, pickled or dried. Chilies can irritate the skin, so it is vital to wash your hands in warm soapy water after handling them. Cooks with particularly sensitive skin should wear gloves.

The tomato is another ingredient essential to Mexican cooking, whether raw or cooked. There is another Mexican green tomato, the tomatillo (*Physalis ixocarpa*), which has

Clockwise from top left: small green chilies, chipotle chilies, mulato chilies, habanero chilies, pasilla chilies, green peppers, green jalapeño chilies, Anaheim chilies, and (center left) Scotch bonnet chilies, (center right) fresh red chilies.

an exquisite flavor. It is widely used in Mexico but is less popular in Guatemala.

The Mexican kitchen is strongly regional. The cattle country of the north, bordering Texas, is not good corn country, and here the wheat flour tortilla is popular. It is often eaten with roasted baby goat, which is a northern favorite.

Much of the lower country is at an altitude of 7–8000 feet. In these regions the climate is temperate, and all kinds of fruits and vegetables flourish on the high plateau.

The semi-tropical regions at sea level have abundant tropical fruits and vegetables, including papayas, pineapples and coconuts. The extensive coastline yields a rich harvest of fish and shellfish. Before the Aztecs dominated the country, the Mayan Empire had flourished, invading Mexico's Yucatán peninsula and the southern part of the country. Here the cooking is subtly different. There are many regional chilies as well as unique herbs and spices. *Achiote* (annatto) is especially popular. The area boasts a sauce, *ixni-pec* (pronounced Schnee-peck), made with the *habanero* chili – the hottest chili in North America.

The ancient art of cooking in an earth oven still flourishes in Mexico. For *barbacoa* in the plateau, a pit is lined with the leaves of the agave plant. Heated stones are placed in the pit,

the food (a whole lamb, vegetables and so on) is arranged on top, the pit is sealed, and the food is left to cook. The agave lends a subtle flavor of tequila to the food. In the Yucatán, the earth oven is called a *pib*. It is lined with banana leaves, and the meat, a suckling pig or maybe a chicken, is seasoned with achiote, among other flavorings, and sprinkled with Seville orange juice, before being sealed in the pit and cooked.

In spite of industrialization, most people in Mexico prefer to eat their main meal, the *comida*, in the middle of the day. This is a long, late lunch, often followed by a siesta. Soup is a must and so are beans. A small dish of beans (usually red kidney or pinto) is served separately after the main course and before dessert, which is often just fresh fruit. Breakfast is coffee with milk and a sweet roll. *Almuerzo*, a light meal which often bridges the gap between breakfast and *comida*, usually consists of a corn-based dish, and although there may be a proper dinner, *cena*, served very late, more often the last meal of the day is a light supper, *merienda*. This is often comprised of tamales (a minced meat and corn dish) and atole (corn gruel), with perhaps the addition of a few sweet rolls and some jam.

RED ENCHILADAS

iterally, *enchilada* means "stuffed with chilies." All kinds are very popular snacks in Mexico.

INGREDIENTS
4 dried ancho chilies
1 pound tomatoes, peeled, seeded and chopped
1 onion, finely chopped
1 garlic clove, chopped
1 tablespoon chopped fresh cilantro
corn oil, for frying
1 cup sour cream
4 chorizo sausages, skinned and chopped
18 fresh Corn Tortillas
2½ cups freshly grated Parmesan cheese
salt and freshly ground black pepper

SERVES 6

COOK'S TIP
Dipping the tortillas in sauce, then quickly cooking them in oil, gives the best flavor. If you prefer, fry the plain tortillas very quickly, then dip them in the sauce, stuff and roll. There is not a great loss of flavor, and no spatter.

---

1 Roast the ancho chilies in a dry frying pan over medium heat for 1–2 minutes, shaking the pan frequently. When cool, carefully slit the chilies, remove the stems and seeds, and tear the pods into pieces. Put in a bowl, add warm water just to cover, and soak for 20 minutes.

2 Pour the chilies, with a little of the soaking water, into a food processor. Add the tomatoes, onion, garlic and cilantro; purée.

3 Heat 1 tablespoon of oil in a frying pan. Add the purée and cook gently over medium heat, stirring, for 3–4 minutes. Season to taste with salt and pepper and stir in the sour cream. Remove from the heat and set aside.

4 Heat an additional 1 tablespoon of oil in a small frying pan; sauté the chorizo for a few minutes until lightly browned. Moisten with a little sauce and set the pan aside.

5 Preheat the oven to 350°F. Heat 2 tablespoons of oil in a frying pan. Dip a tortilla in the sauce. Add to the pan and cook for a few seconds, shaking the pan gently. Turn over and repeat.

6 Slide the tortilla onto a plate, top with some sausage mixture, and roll up. Pack in a single layer in a baking dish. Pour the sauce on top, sprinkle with Parmesan and bake for about 20 minutes.

CORN
TORTILLAS

ave ready a tortilla press and a small plastic bag, cut open along the seams.

INGREDIENTS
2 cups masa harina
(tortilla flour)
1–1½ cups water

MAKES ABOUT FOURTEEN
5½-INCH TORTILLAS

1 Put the *masa harina* into a bowl and stir in 1 cup of the water, making a soft dough that just holds together. If it is too dry, add a little more water. If too wet, add more *masa harina*. Cover with a cloth and set aside for 15 minutes.

COOK'S TIP
Tortillas are easy to make, but it is important to get the dough texture right. If it is too crumbly, add a little water; if it is too wet, add more *masa harina*. If you misjudge the pressure needed for flattening the ball of dough to a neat circle on the press, just scrape it off, re-roll it and try again.

2 Preheat the oven to 300°F. Open the tortilla press and line both sides with the prepared plastic sheets. Preheat a griddle until hot.

3 Knead the dough lightly and shape into 14 balls. Put a ball on the press and bring the top down firmly to flatten the dough out into a circle.

4 Open the press. Peel off the top layer of plastic and lift the tortilla with the bottom plastic. Turn it onto your palm, so the plastic is on top. Peel off the plastic and flip the tortilla onto the hot griddle.

5 Cook for about 1 minute, or until the edges start to curl. Turn over and cook for another minute. Wrap in foil and keep warm.

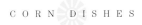

FLOUR TORTILLAS

ssential for stuffing, filling and wrapping all kinds of foods, tortillas are basic to Mexican cuisine.

INGREDIENTS
2 cups flour
1 teaspoon salt
1 tablespoon vegetable shortening
½ cup water

MAKES ABOUT FOURTEEN
6-INCH TORTILLAS

1 Sift the flour and salt into a mixing bowl. Rub in the shortening with your fingertips until the mixture resembles coarse bread crumbs.

2 Gradually add the water and mix into a soft dough. Knead lightly, form into a ball, cover the bowl with a cloth and let rest for 15 minutes.

3 Divide the dough into about 14 portions and form into balls. On a lightly floured board, roll out each ball of dough into a 6-inch circle. Trim the circles if necessary.

4 Heat a medium, ungreased griddle or heavy frying pan over medium heat. Cook the tortillas, one at a time, for about 1½–2 minutes on each side. Turn over with a large spatula when the bottom becomes a delicate brown. Adjust the heat if the tortilla browns too quickly.

5 Stack the tortillas in a clean cloth if eating right away. Otherwise, wrap in foil and keep warm in the oven.

COOK'S TIP
Make flour tortillas if *masa harina* is hard to find. To keep them soft and pliable, make sure they are kept warm.

TACOS

The taco has been called the Mexican sandwich; it is eaten in the hand, making a great, speedy snack. All you need is a supply of tortillas or taco shells and a selection of fillings.

INGREDIENTS
freshly prepared Corn Tortillas
or prepared taco shells

FOR THE FILLINGS
Picadillo, topped with guacamole
chopped chorizo, fried and mixed
with chopped Cheddar cheese
and chilies
Refried Beans (frijoles refritos),
with sliced jalapeño chilies,
guacamole and cubed cheese
leftover Mole Poblano de Guajolote
with guacamole
cooked shredded pork or chicken
with salsa and shredded lettuce

MAKES AS MANY AS YOU LIKE

COOK'S TIP
Filo pastry dries out very quickly and then becomes impossible to work with. Cover with a damp dish towel and take out one sheet at a time.

1 To make tacos, all you need is a supply of fresh corn tortillas and as many of the suggested fillings as you desire. The idea is to use your imagination, and cooks often vie with one another to see who can produce the most interesting combination of flavors. Chilies and guacamole are always welcome, in the taco or served as an accompaniment.

2 To make traditional soft tacos, simply spoon the filling onto the tortilla, wrap the tortilla around the filling – and eat.

3 To make hard tacos, secure the rolled up, filled tortilla with a toothpick, then briefly fry until crisp and golden.

4 Prepared U-shaped taco shells are not Mexican, but make a great speedy version of this snack. Hold one taco shell at a time in one hand, and fill with the fillings of your choice.

TORTILLA FLUTES

F lutes, or *flautas*, look as good as they taste and are particularly delicious accompanied by salsa, which can be found in most supermarkets.

INGREDIENTS
24 freshly prepared unbaked
Flour Tortillas
2 tomatoes, peeled, seeded and chopped
1 small onion, chopped
1 garlic clove, chopped
2–3 tablespoons corn oil
2 freshly cooked chicken breasts,
skinned and shredded
salt
sliced radishes and stuffed green olives,
to garnish

MAKES ABOUT 12

1 Place the unbaked tortillas in pairs on a work surface, with the right-hand tortilla overlapping its partner by about 2 inches.

2 Process the tomatoes, onion and garlic to a purée. Season with salt to taste. Heat 1 tablespoon of the oil in a frying pan and cook the tomato purée for a few minutes, stirring to blend the flavors. Remove from the heat and stir in the shredded chicken, mixing well.

3 Spread about 2 tablespoons of the chicken mixture on each pair of tortillas, roll them up into flutes and secure with a toothpick.

4 Heat a little oil in a frying pan large enough to hold the flutes. Cook more than one at a time if possible, but don't overcrowd the pan. Fry the flutes until light brown all over. Add more oil if necessary.

5 Drain the cooked flutes on paper towels, and keep hot. When ready to serve, transfer to a platter and garnish with radishes and olives.

CORN SOUP

This is a simple-to-make yet very flavorful soup. It can also be made with sour cream and cream cheese instead of light cream.

INGREDIENTS
2 tablespoons corn oil
1 onion, finely chopped
1 red bell pepper, seeded and chopped
1 pound corn kernels,
thawed if frozen
3 cups chicken stock
1 cup light cream
salt and freshly ground black pepper
½ red bell pepper, seeded and
diced, to garnish

SERVES 4

1 Heat the oil in a frying pan and sauté the onion and bell pepper until soft, for about 5 minutes. Add the corn and sauté for 2 minutes.

2 Carefully pour the contents of the pan into a food processor or blender. Process until smooth, scraping down the sides and adding a little of the stock, if necessary.

3 Put the mixture into a saucepan and stir in the stock. Season to taste with salt and pepper, bring to a simmer and cook for 5 minutes.

4 Gently stir in the cream. Serve the soup hot or chilled, sprinkled with the diced red pepper. If serving hot, reheat gently before adding the cream, but do not allow the soup to boil.

COOK'S TIP
Reheat the soup thoroughly, remove from heat and add the cream. Don't stir the cream in completely; a few streaks and swirls look very pretty.

AVOCADO SOUP

Avocado makes a delicious and creamy soup, which is beautifully complemented by fresh cilantro. Serve either hot or cold.

INGREDIENTS
2 large ripe avocados
4 cups chicken stock
1 cup light cream or half-and-half
salt and freshly ground white pepper
1 tablespoon finely chopped cilantro,
to garnish (optional)

SERVES 4

1 Cut the avocados in half, remove the pits and mash the flesh. Put it into a strainer and, with a wooden spoon, press it through into a warm soup bowl.

2 Heat the chicken stock with the cream in a saucepan over low heat. When the mixture is hot, but not boiling, whisk it into the puréed avocado.

3 Season to taste with salt and white pepper. Serve immediately, sprinkled with the cilantro, if desired. The soup may also be served chilled.

COOK'S TIP
The easiest way to mash avocados is to hold each pitted half in the palm of one hand and mash the flesh in the shell with a fork, before scooping it into the bowl. This prevents the avocado from slithering around while it is being mashed.

TOMATO SOUP

 Many cuisines offer a tomato soup, and Mexico's is deliciously fresh and simple.

INGREDIENTS

1 tablespoon corn or peanut oil
1 onion, finely chopped
*2 pounds tomatoes, peeled, seeded
and chopped*
2 cups chicken stock
2 large fresh cilantro sprigs
salt and freshly ground black pepper
coarsely ground black pepper, to serve

SERVES 4

1 Heat the oil in a large saucepan and gently fry the finely chopped onion, stirring frequently, for about 5 minutes, or until the onion becomes soft and transparent but not brown.

2 Add the chopped tomatoes, chicken stock and cilantro sprigs to the pan. Bring to a boil, then lower the heat, cover the pan and let the soup simmer gently for about 15 minutes.

3 Remove and discard the cilantro sprigs. Press the soup through a strainer and return it to the clean saucepan. Season to taste and heat through. Serve sprinkled with coarsely ground black pepper.

MEXICAN-STYLE RICE

ice, aside from tortillas, is the most popular accompaniment for Mexican food.

INGREDIENTS
1¾ cups long-grain white rice
1 onion, chopped
2 garlic cloves, chopped
1 pound tomatoes, peeled, seeded and coarsely chopped
4 tablespoons corn or peanut oil
3¾ cups chicken stock
1 cup cooked green peas
salt and freshly ground black pepper
4–6 small red chilies and
fresh cilantro sprigs, to garnish

SERVES 6

1 Soak the rice in a bowl of hot water for 15 minutes. Drain, rinse well under cold running water, drain again and set aside.

2 Combine the onion, garlic and tomatoes in a food processor and process.

3 Heat the oil in a large frying pan. Add the drained rice and sauté until golden brown. Using a slotted spoon, transfer the rice to a saucepan.

4 Reheat the oil remaining in the pan and cook the tomato paste for 2–3 minutes. Pour it into the saucepan and add the stock. Season to taste. Bring to a boil, reduce the heat as low as possible, cover the pan and cook for 15–20 minutes, until almost all the liquid has been absorbed.

5 Stir the peas into the rice mixture and cook, without a lid, until all the liquid has been absorbed and the rice is tender. Stir the mixture occasionally.

6 Transfer the rice to a serving dish and garnish with the drained chili flowers (see Cook's Tip) and sprigs of cilantro. Warn the diners that these elaborate chili flowers are hot and should be approached with much caution.

COOK'S TIP
Slice the red chilies from tip to stem end into four or five sections. Place in a bowl of ice water until they curl back to form flowers, then drain.

REFRIED BEANS

There is much disagreement about the translation of the term *refrito*. It means, literally, "twice fried." Some cooks say this implies that the beans must be really well fried, others that it means twice cooked. Whatever it means, *Frijoles Refritos* are delicious.

INGREDIENTS
6–8 tablespoons vegetable shortening or corn oil
1 onion, finely chopped
1 quantity frijoles
(cooked beans)

TO GARNISH
freshly grated Parmesan cheese or crumbled Farmers cheese
crisp fried corn tortillas, cut into quarters

SERVES 6–8

1 Heat 2 tablespoons of the fat in a large heavy frying pan and sauté the onion until it is soft. Add 1 cup of the *frijoles* (cooked beans).

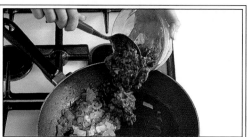

2 Mash the beans with the back of a wooden spoon or potato masher, adding more beans and melted fat until all the ingredients are used up and the beans have formed a heavy paste. Use extra fat if necessary.

3 Transfer the beans to a warmed platter, piling the mixture up in a roll. Garnish with the cheese. Spike with the tortilla triangles, placing them at intervals along the length of the roll. Serve as a side dish.

COOK'S TIP
Lard is the traditional (and best-tasting) fat in which to cook the beans, but many people prefer to use corn oil. Avoid using olive oil, which is too strongly flavored and distinctive.

CHAYOTE SALAD

C hayote goes by several different names – *chocho*, christophine or vegetable pear being the most common. Native to Mexico, they are now widely cultivated in the Caribbean, Southeast Asia and parts of Africa.

INGREDIENTS

2 chayotes, peeled and halved
1 large beefsteak tomato, about 8 ounces,
peeled and cut into 6 wedges
1 small onion, finely chopped

FOR THE DRESSING

½ teaspoon Dijon mustard
2 tablespoons white vinegar
6 tablespoons olive or corn oil
salt and freshly ground black pepper
strips of seeded pickled jalapeño chilies,
to garnish

SERVES 4

COOK'S TIP
The seed of the chayote is edible and makes an admirable cook's perk.

1 Without removing the seeds, cook the chayotes in a large saucepan of boiling salted water for about 20 minutes or until tender. Drain and let cool. Remove the seeds and set them aside (see Cook's Tip). Cut the flesh into chunks about the same size as the tomato wedges.

2 Make the dressing in a salad bowl. Combine the mustard and vinegar with salt and pepper to taste. Gradually whisk in the oil until well combined.

3 Put the chayote chunks, tomato wedges and finely chopped onion in the bowl. Toss gently with the dressing until everything is well coated.

4 Put in a serving dish, garnish with the chili strips and serve.

PEPPERS STUFFED WITH BEANS

Stuffed peppers are a popular Mexican dish. A special version – *Chiles en Nogada* – is served every year on August 28 to celebrate Independence Day. The green peppers are served with a sauce of fresh walnuts and a garnish of pomegranate seeds to represent the colors of the Mexican flag.

INGREDIENTS
6 large green bell peppers
1 recipe Refried Beans
2 eggs, separated
½ teaspoon salt
corn oil, for frying
flour, for dusting
½ cup whipping cream
1 cup grated Cheddar cheese
fresh cilantro sprigs, to garnish

SERVES 6

1 Roast the peppers over a gas flame or under a broiler, turning occasionally, until the skins have blackened and blistered. Transfer the peppers to a plastic bag, secure the top and set aside for 15 minutes.

2 Preheat the oven to 350°F. Remove the peppers from the bag. Hold each pepper under cold running water and gently rub off the skins. Slit the peppers down one side and remove the seeds and ribs, taking care not to break the pepper shells. Stuff with the refried beans.

3 Beat the egg whites in a large bowl until they stand in stiff peaks. In another bowl, beat the yolks lightly together with the salt. Fold the yolks gently into the whites.

4 Pour the corn oil into a large frying pan to a depth of about 1 inch and heat. Spread out the flour in a shallow bowl or on a flat plate.

5 Dip the filled peppers in the flour and then in the egg mixture. Fry in batches in the hot oil until golden brown all over. Arrange the peppers in an ovenproof dish. Pour the cream on top and sprinkle them with the cheese. Bake for 30 minutes, or until the topping is golden brown and the peppers are heated through. Serve at once, garnished with fresh cilantro.

GREEN LIMA BEANS IN SAUCE

tasty and wholesome dish of lima beans, cooked in a tomato and chili sauce.

INGREDIENTS
1 pound green lima or fava beans,
thawed if frozen
2 tablespoons olive oil
1 onion, finely chopped
2 garlic cloves, chopped
12 ounces tomatoes, peeled,
seeded and chopped
1 or 2 drained canned jalapeño
chilies, seeded and chopped
salt
fresh cilantro sprigs, to garnish

SERVES 4

1 Cook the beans in a saucepan of boiling water for 15–20 minutes or until tender. Drain and keep hot in the covered saucepan.

2 Heat the olive oil in a frying pan and sauté the onion and garlic until the onion is soft but not brown. Add the tomatoes and cook until the mixture is rich and thick.

3 Add the jalapeños and cook for 1–2 more minutes. Season with salt.

4 Pour the mixture over the reserved beans and check that they are hot. If not, return everything to the frying pan and cook over low heat for just long enough to heat through. Put into a warm serving dish, garnish with the cilantro and serve.

CHOPPED ZUCCHINI

*C*alabacitas is an extremely easy recipe to make. If the cooking time seems unduly long, this is because the acid in the tomatoes slows down the cooking of the zucchini.

INGREDIENTS
2 tablespoons corn oil
1 pound young zucchini, sliced
1 onion, finely chopped
2 garlic cloves, chopped
1 pound tomatoes, peeled,
seeded and chopped
2 drained canned jalapeño chilies,
rinsed, seeded and chopped
1 tablespoon chopped fresh cilantro
salt
fresh cilantro sprigs, to garnish

SERVES 4

1 Heat the oil in a flameproof casserole and add all the remaining ingredients, except the salt and cilantro sprigs.

2 Bring to a simmer, cover and cook over low heat for 30 minutes, or until the zucchini is tender. Check occasionally to make sure that the dish is not drying out; if it is, add a little tomato juice, stock or water.

3 Season with salt and serve the Mexican way – as a separate course. Alternatively, serve accompanied by any simply cooked meat or poultry dish. Garnish with fresh cilantro sprigs.

FRIJOLES

This basic method for cooking dried beans is the starting point for refried beans.

INGREDIENTS
1¼–1½ cups dried red kidney, pinto or black beans, picked over and rinsed
2 onions, finely chopped
2 garlic cloves, chopped
1 bay leaf
1 or more serrano chilies (or other small fresh green chilies)
2 tablespoons corn oil
2 tomatoes, peeled, seeded and chopped
salt
sprigs of fresh bay leaves, to garnish

SERVES 6–8

COOK'S TIP
In the Yucatán, black beans are often cooked with the Mexican herb *epazote*.

1 Put the beans in a pan and add cold water to cover by 1 inch.

2 Add half the onion, half the garlic, the bay leaf and the chili(es). Bring to a boil and cook vigorously for 10 minutes. Put the beans and liquid into an earthenware pot or large saucepan, cover and cook over low heat for 30 minutes. Add boiling water if the mixture starts to become dry.

3 When the beans begin to wrinkle, add 1 tablespoon of the corn oil and cook for 30 more minutes or until the beans are tender. Add salt to taste and cook for 30 more minutes, without adding water.

4 Remove the beans from the heat. Heat the remaining oil in a small frying pan and sauté the rest of the onion and garlic until the onion is soft. Add the tomatoes and cook for a few more minutes.

5 Spoon 3 tablespoons of the beans out of the pot or pan and add them to the tomato mixture. Mash to a paste. Stir this into the beans to thicken the liquid. Cook just long enough to heat through, if necessary. Serve the beans in small bowls and garnish with sprigs of fresh bay leaves.

AVOCADO AND TOMATO SALAD

A refreshing salad to accompany spicy dishes. To ripen avocados, put them in a brown paper bag and store in a dark place for several days, checking occasionally. They are ready when they yield to gentle pressure at the stem end.

INGREDIENTS
2 ripe avocados
2 large beefsteak tomatoes, about
8 ounces each, peeled and seeded
1 head Iceberg lettuce, coarsely shredded,
or mixed salad leaves
2 tablespoons chopped fresh cilantro
salt and freshly ground black pepper

FOR THE DRESSING
6 tablespoons olive or corn oil
2 tablespoons fresh lemon juice

SERVES 4

1 Cut the avocados in half, remove the pits and peel off the skin. Then cut the avocados and tomatoes into equal numbers of slices of approximately the same size.

2 Arrange a bed of shredded lettuce on a large platter and place the tomato slices on top. Arrange the avocado slices over the tomato and sprinkle with the cilantro. Season to taste with salt and pepper.

3 To make the dressing, whisk the olive oil and lemon juice together in a bowl until well combined.

4 Pour a little dressing over the salad and serve the rest separately.

SHRIMP SALAD

S alads in Mexico are usually served with the main course instead of green vegetables. Salads containing meat or seafood are served as a separate course, because they are very filling.

INGREDIENTS
1 head Iceberg lettuce
or assorted lettuce leaves
¼ cup mayonnaise
¼ cup sour cream
12 ounces cooked shrimp,
thawed if frozen, chopped
½ cup cooked
green beans, chopped
½ cup cooked carrots, chopped
½ cucumber, about 4 ounces, chopped
2 hard-cooked eggs, coarsely chopped
1 drained pickled jalapeño chili,
seeded and chopped
salt

SERVES 4

COOK'S TIP
Use crisp-leaved lettuce for a delightful contrast of texture with the other ingredients.

1 Line a large salad bowl or platter with the lettuce leaves. Combine the mayonnaise and sour cream in a small bowl and set aside.

2 Combine the shrimp, beans, carrots, cucumber, eggs and chili in a separate bowl. Season with salt.

3 Add the mayonnaise and sour cream mixture to the shrimp, folding it in very gently so that all the shrimp are thoroughly coated with the dressing. Pile the mixture into the lined salad bowl or arrange attractively on the platter and serve.

RED SNAPPER, VERACRUZ-STYLE

This is Mexico's best-known fish dish. In Veracruz, red snapper is always used for this recipe but fillets of any firm-fleshed white fish can be substituted successfully.

INGREDIENTS

4 large red snapper fillets
2 tablespoons freshly squeezed lime
or lemon juice
½ cup olive oil
1 onion, finely chopped
2 garlic cloves, chopped
1½ pounds tomatoes,
peeled and chopped
1 bay leaf, plus a few sprigs to garnish
¼ teaspoon dried oregano
2 tablespoons large capers, plus extra
to serve (optional)
16 pitted green olives, halved
2 drained canned jalapeño chilies,
seeded and cut into strips
butter, for frying
3 slices firm white bread,
cut into triangles
salt and freshly ground black pepper

SERVES 4

1 Arrange the fish fillets in a single layer in a shallow dish. Season with salt and pepper, drizzle with the lime or lemon juice and set aside.

2 Heat the oil in a large frying pan and sauté the onion and garlic until the onion becomes soft. Add the tomatoes and cook for 10 minutes, or until the mixture is thick and flavorful. Stir the mixture occasionally, to prevent it from sticking to the bottom of the pan.

COOK'S TIP
This dish can also be made with a whole fish, weighing about 3–3½ pounds. Bake together with the sauce, in an oven preheated to 325°F. Allow 10 minutes cooking time for every 1 inch thickness of the fish.

3 Stir in the bay leaf, oregano, capers, olives and chilies. Add the fish and cook over very low heat for about 10 minutes or until tender.

4 While the fish is cooking, heat the butter in a small frying pan and sauté the bread triangles until they are golden brown on both sides.

5 Transfer the fish to a heated platter, pour the sauce on top and surround with the fried bread. Garnish with bay leaves and serve with extra capers, if desired.

CRAB WITH GREEN RICE

This delicious seafood dish is a complete meal because it is served with green rice, an interesting variation on more common rice dishes.

INGREDIENTS

1 cup long-grain rice
4 tablespoons olive oil
2 cans (10 ounces each) tomatillos
(Mexican green tomatoes)
1 onion, chopped
2 garlic cloves, chopped
2 tablespoons chopped fresh cilantro
1½ cups chicken stock
1 pound crabmeat, thawed
if frozen, broken into chunks
salt and freshly ground pepper
chopped fresh cilantro, to garnish
lettuce leaves, to serve

SERVES 4

1 Soak the rice in hot water to cover for 15 minutes; drain thoroughly. Heat the oil in a frying pan and sauté the rice over medium heat, stirring until the rice is golden and the oil has been absorbed.

2 Drain the tomatillos, reserving the juice, and put them into a food processor. Add the onion, garlic and cilantro, and process to a purée. Pour into a 2-cup measure and add the tomatillo juice. Pour in enough stock to make 2 cups. Season to taste.

COOK'S TIP
Mexican cooks always soak rice in water before cooking it. This seems to pay off because their rice is always delicious, with every grain separate.

3 Place the rice, tomato mixture and crabmeat in a shallow pan. Cover and cook over very low heat for about 30 minutes or until the liquid has been absorbed and the rice is tender. Serve on lettuce leaves, garnished with chopped fresh cilantro.

SHRIMP WITH PUMPKIN SEED SAUCE

 round pumpkin seeds give the sauce for this shrimp dish a delicious and unusual texture.

INGREDIENTS

1 generous cup pepitas (Mexican pumpkin seeds)

1 pound raw shrimp, thawed if frozen, peeled and deveined

1 onion, chopped

1 garlic clove, chopped

2 tablespoons chopped fresh cilantro

8 ounces tomatoes, peeled and chopped

1 drained canned jalapeño chili, rinsed, seeded and chopped

1 red bell pepper, seeded and chopped

2 tablespoons corn oil

salt

whole cooked shrimp, lemon slices and fresh cilantro sprigs, to garnish

rice, to serve

SERVES 4

1 Grind the pumpkin seeds finely and shake through a strainer into a bowl. Set aside.

2 Cook the shrimp in boiling salted water. As soon as they turn pink, remove with a slotted spoon and set them aside. Reserve the cooking water.

3 Purée the onion, garlic, cilantro, tomatoes, chili, red bell pepper and pumpkin seeds in a food processor. Heat the oil in a pan, stir and cook the mixture for 5 minutes. Season with salt. Add shrimp water to thin the mixture to a sauce consistency. Heat gently and add the shrimp. Garnish with cilantro sprigs, and serve with rice.

SEVICHE

This dish makes an excellent opener for a summer meal. With the addition of sliced avocado, it could also make a light lunch for four.

INGREDIENTS

*1 pound mackerel or red snapper fillets,
cut into ½-inch pieces
1½ cups freshly squeezed lime or
lemon juice
8 ounces tomatoes, chopped
1 small onion, very finely chopped
2 drained canned jalapeño chilies or
4 serrano chilies, rinsed and chopped
4 tablespoons olive oil
½ teaspoon dried oregano
2 tablespoons chopped fresh cilantro
salt and freshly ground black pepper
lemon wedges and fresh cilantro,
to garnish
stuffed green olives, to serve*

SERVES 6

1 Put the fish into a glass dish and pour the citrus juice over it, making sure that the fish is totally covered. Cover and chill for 6 hours, turning once, by which time the fish will be opaque, "cooked" by the juice.

2 When the fish is opaque, lift it out of the juice and set it aside, reserving the juice.

COOK'S TIP
For a more delicately flavored Seviche,
use scallops instead of mackerel.

3 Combine the tomatoes, onion, chilies, olive oil, oregano and cilantro in a bowl. Add salt and pepper to taste, then pour in the reserved juice from the mackerel. Mix well and pour over the fish.

4 Cover the dish and return the Seviche to the fridge for about an hour to allow the flavors to blend. Seviche should not be served too cold. Allow it to stand at room temperature for 15 minutes before serving. Garnish with lemon wedges and cilantro sprigs, and serve with stuffed green olives sprinkled with chopped cilantro.

SHRIMP IN SAUCE

his colorful dish is called *Camarones en Salsa* in Mexico – serve it with rice, if desired.

INGREDIENTS
4 tablespoons olive or corn oil
1 red bell pepper, seeded and chopped
2 large scallions (white and green parts), chopped
2 garlic cloves, chopped
1 pound tomatoes, peeled, seeded and chopped
4 tablespoons chopped fresh cilantro
a little chicken stock
1 pound raw or cooked shrimp, thawed if frozen, peeled and deveined
salt and freshly ground black pepper
fresh cilantro, to garnish

SERVES 4

1 Heat the oil in a flameproof casserole and sauté the pepper, scallions and garlic until the pepper is soft. Add the tomatoes and simmer for about 10 minutes or until the mixture is thick.

2 Add the cilantro and salt and pepper to taste. If the sauce is very thick, thin with chicken stock.

3 Add the shrimp and cook for 2–3 minutes, depending on the size, until they turn pink. Be very careful not to overcook the shrimp as they will toughen very quickly. Serve immediately, with rice if desired, and garnish with fresh cilantro.

FISH IN
PARSLEY SAUCE

A simple, quick-to-make, delicious fish dish. Try to use flat-leaf or Italian parsley, which has much more flavor than curly parsley.

INGREDIENTS

1 can (10 ounces) tomatillos
(Mexican green tomatoes)
1 onion, finely chopped
2 garlic cloves, chopped
1 cup flat-leaf parsley,
finely chopped
4 tablespoons olive oil
6 firm-fleshed white fish fillets
salt and freshly ground black pepper

TO GARNISH

drained canned serrano chilies,
seeded, rinsed and shredded
sliced black olives

SERVES 6

1 Drain the tomatillos, reserving the liquid. Mash them in a bowl with the onion, garlic and parsley. Season with salt and pepper and set aside.

2 Heat the oil in a large frying pan and sauté the fish fillets until they are golden on both sides. Using a long spatula, transfer the fillets to a warmed serving dish, cover and keep hot.

3 Heat the remaining oil in the pan and add the tomatillo mixture. Cook over medium heat, stirring occasionally, until the sauce is well blended and has the consistency of light cream. If it is too thick, add a little of the reserved tomatillo juice. Season to taste with salt and pepper.

4 Pour the sauce over the fish fillets, garnish with the serrano chilies and black olives and serve.

SALT COD IN MILD CHILI SAUCE

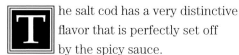 he salt cod has a very distinctive flavor that is perfectly set off by the spicy sauce.

INGREDIENTS
2 pounds dried salt cod

FOR THE SAUCE
6 dried ancho chilies
1 onion, chopped
½ teaspoon dried oregano
½ teaspoon ground coriander
1 serrano chili, seeded and chopped
3 tablespoons corn oil
3 cups fish or
chicken stock
1 fresh green chili, sliced, to garnish

SERVES 6

COOK'S TIP
Dried salt cod is very popular in Spain and Portugal and throughout Latin America. Look for it in Spanish and Portuguese markets.

1 Soak the cod in cold water for several hours, depending on how hard and salty it is. Change the water once or twice during soaking to reduce the saltiness.

2 Drain the fish and transfer it to a saucepan. Pour in water to cover. Bring to a gentle simmer and cook for 15 minutes, until tender. Drain, reserving the stock. Remove any skin or bones from the fish and cut it into 1½-inch pieces.

3 Remove the stems and shake out the seeds from the ancho chilies. Tear the pods into pieces, put them in a bowl of warm water and soak until they are soft.

4 Drain the soaked chilies and put them into a food processor with the onion, oregano, coriander and serrano chili. Process to a purée.

5 Heat the oil in a frying pan and cook the purée, stirring, for about 5 minutes. Stir in the fish stock and simmer for about 3–4 minutes.

6 Add the prepared cod and simmer for a few more minutes to heat the fish through and blend the flavors. Serve garnished with the sliced green chili.

MOLE POBLANO DE GUAJOLOTE

ice, frijoles, tortillas and guacamole traditionally accompany this delicious, festive dish.

INGREDIENTS
6–8 pounds turkey pieces
1 onion and 1 garlic clove, chopped
6 tablespoons corn oil
fresh cilantro and 2 tablespoons
toasted sesame seeds, to garnish

FOR THE SAUCE
6 dried ancho chilies
4 each dried pasilla and mulato chilies
1 drained canned chipotle chili,
seeded and chopped (optional)
2 onions and 2 garlic cloves, chopped
1 pound tomatoes, peeled and chopped
1 stale tortilla, torn into pieces
$\frac{1}{3}$ cup seedless raisins
1 cup ground almonds
1 teaspoon ground cinnamon
$\frac{1}{2}$ teaspoon ground anise
$\frac{1}{4}$ teaspoon ground black peppercorns
4 tablespoons corn oil
$1\frac{1}{2}$ ounces unsweetened chocolate
1 tablespoon sugar
salt and freshly ground pepper
3 tablespoons sesame seeds, ground
$\frac{1}{2}$ teaspoon coriander seeds, ground

SERVES 6–8

1 Put the turkey pieces into a saucepan or flameproof casserole large enough to hold them in one layer comfortably. Add the onion and garlic and cold water to cover. Season with salt, bring to a gentle simmer, cover and cook for 1 hour or until tender.

2 Meanwhile, put the ancho, pasilla and mulato chilies in a dry frying pan over gentle heat and roast them for a few minutes, shaking the pan frequently. Remove the stems and shake out the seeds. Tear the pods into pieces and put them into a small bowl. Add enough warm water to just cover and soak, turning occasionally, for 30 minutes, until soft.

3 Dry the turkey pieces with paper towels. Reserve the stock. Heat the oil in a large frying pan and sauté the turkey until lightly browned all over. Set aside. Reserve the oil.

4 Pour the chilies, with the water in which they have been soaked, into a food processor. Add the chipotle chili, if using, with the onions, garlic, tomatoes, tortilla, raisins, ground almonds and spices. Process to a purée. Do this in batches if necessary.

5 Add the oil to the fat remaining in the frying pan. Heat the mixture, then add the chili and spice paste. Cook, stirring, for 5 minutes.

6 Transfer the mixture to the pan or casserole in which the turkey was originally cooked. Stir in 2 cups of the turkey stock (add water if necessary). Chop and add the chocolate, and season with salt and pepper. Cook over low heat until the chocolate has melted. Stir in the sugar. Add the turkey and more stock if necessary. Cover the pan and simmer very gently for 30 minutes. Garnish with cilantro and sesame seeds, and serve.

PICADILLO

Serve as a main dish with rice, or use this versatile recipe to stuff peppers or fill tacos.

INGREDIENTS
2 tablespoons olive or corn oil
2 pounds ground beef
1 onion, finely chopped
2 garlic cloves, chopped
2 eating apples
1 pound tomatoes, peeled,
seeded and chopped
2 or 3 drained pickled jalapeño
chilies, seeded and chopped
scant ½ cup raisins
¼ teaspoon ground cinnamon
¼ teaspoon ground cumin
salt and freshly ground black pepper

TO GARNISH
1 tablespoon butter
¼ cup slivered almonds
tortilla chips, to serve

SERVES 6

1 Heat the oil in a large frying pan and add the beef, onion and garlic. Fry, stirring occasionally, until the beef is brown and the onion is tender.

COOK'S TIP
Keep stirring the ground beef while it's browning, to break up any lumps.

2 Peel, core and chop the apples. Add them to the pan with all the remaining ingredients, except the garnishes and tortilla chips. Cook, uncovered, for 20–25 minutes, stirring occasionally.

3 Just before serving, melt the butter in a small frying pan and sauté the almonds until golden brown. Serve the picadillo topped with the almonds and accompanied by the tortilla chips.

VEAL IN NUT SAUCE

round nuts and sour cream combine to make an unusual sauce for veal.

INGREDIENTS
3–3½ pound boneless veal,
cut into 2-inch cubes
2 onions, finely chopped
1 garlic clove, crushed
½ teaspoon dried thyme
½ teaspoon dried oregano
1½ cups chicken stock
¾ cup very finely ground almonds,
pecans or peanuts
¾ cup sour cream
fresh oregano sprigs, to garnish
rice, to serve

SERVES 6

COOK'S TIP
Choose domestically raised pink veal if you can. It has a better flavor and tends to be more moist than white veal.

1 Put the cubes of veal, finely chopped onions, crushed garlic, thyme, oregano and chicken stock into a large flameproof casserole. Bring to a gentle boil. Cover tightly and simmer slowly over a low heat for about 2 hours, until the veal is cooked and tender.

2 Put the ground nuts in a food processor. Pour in ½ cup of the veal liquid and process for a few seconds until smooth. Press through a strainer straight into the casserole.

3 Stir in the sour cream and heat through gently, without boiling. Garnish with oregano. Serve immediately with rice.

MEATBALLS

Mexican cooks use twice-ground beef and pork for *albondigas*. If preferred, the meatballs can be simply poached in beef stock.

INGREDIENTS
8 ounces lean ground beef
8 ounces ground pork
1 cup fresh white bread crumbs
1 onion, finely chopped
½ teaspoon dried oregano
or ground cumin
corn oil, for frying
1 egg, lightly beaten
milk (optional)
salt and freshly ground black pepper
oregano leaves, to garnish

FOR THE SAUCE
beef stock
1 chipotle chili, seeded and chopped
1 onion, finely chopped
2 garlic cloves, crushed
8 ounces tomatoes, peeled, seeded and
finely chopped

SERVES 4

1 Put the beef and pork through a meat grinder or process in a food processor, if it is not already finely minced. Transfer it to a bowl and add the bread crumbs, onion and oregano. Season with salt and pepper and stir in the egg.

2 Knead thoroughly with clean hands to make a smooth mixture, adding a little milk if necessary. Shape the mixture into 1½-inch balls.

3 Heat ½ inch oil in a frying pan and fry the balls for 5 minutes, turning occasionally, until browned.

4 Put the meatballs in a shallow pan or flameproof casserole and add beef stock to cover. Add the remaining sauce ingredients and bring to a boil. Simmer for about 30 minutes. Using a slotted spoon, transfer the meatballs to a serving dish. Press the sauce through a strainer then spoon it over the meatballs. Serve immediately, garnished with oregano leaves.

LAMB STEW

This stew is known as *estofado de carnero* in Mexico. It has an interesting mix of chilies – the mild, full-flavored ancho, and the piquant jalapeño, which gives extra bite. The heat of the chilies is mellowed by the addition of ground cinnamon and cloves.

INGREDIENTS
3 dried ancho chilies
2 tablespoons olive oil
1 jalapeño chili, seeded and chopped
1 onion, finely chopped
2 garlic cloves, chopped
1 pound tomatoes, peeled and chopped
1/3 cup seedless raisins
1/4 teaspoon ground cinnamon
1/4 teaspoon ground cloves
2 pounds boneless lamb,
cut into 2-inch cubes
1 cup lamb stock or water
salt and freshly ground black pepper
a few sprigs of fresh cilantro, to garnish
rice, with herbs, to serve

SERVES 4

1 Roast the ancho chilies lightly in a dry frying pan over low heat. This will bring out their flavor.

2 Remove the stems, shake out the seeds, tear the pods into pieces and put them in a bowl. Pour in enough warm water just to cover. Let soak for 30 minutes.

3 Heat the olive oil in a frying pan and sauté the jalapeño chili with the onion and garlic until the onion becomes soft and tender.

4 Add the chopped tomatoes to the pan and cook until the mixture is thick and well blended. Stir in the raisins, ground cinnamon and cloves, and season to taste with salt and ground black pepper. Transfer the mixture to a flameproof casserole.

5 Pour the ancho chilies and their soaking water into a food processor and process to a smooth purée. Add the chili purée to the tomato mixture in the casserole.

6 Add the cubed lamb to the casserole, stir to mix and pour in enough of the lamb stock or water to just cover the meat.

7 Bring to a simmer, then cover the casserole and cook over low heat for about 2 hours or until the lamb is tender. Garnish with fresh cilantro and serve with rice mixed with herbs.

CHICKEN IN GREEN ALMOND SAUCE

he bright green sauce, with the elusive flavor of almonds, complements the chicken.

INGREDIENTS

1 chicken (3–3¹/₂ pounds),
cut into serving pieces
2 cups chicken stock
1 onion, chopped
1 garlic clove, chopped
2 cups fresh cilantro,
coarsely chopped
1 green bell pepper, seeded and chopped
1 jalapeño chili, seeded and chopped
1 can (10 ounces) tomatillos
(Mexican green tomatoes)
1 cup ground almonds
2 tablespoons corn oil
salt
fresh cilantro, to garnish
rice, to serve

SERVES 6

COOK'S TIP

If the sauce seems a little pale, add 2–3 outer leaves of dark green Romaine lettuce. Cut out the central veins, chop the leaves and add to the food processor with the other ingredients.

1 Put the chicken pieces into a flameproof casserole or shallow pan. Pour in the stock, bring to a simmer, cover and cook for about 45 minutes, until tender. Drain the stock into a 2-cup measure and set aside.

2 Put the onion, garlic, cilantro, bell pepper, chili, tomatillos with their juice and the almonds in a food processor. Purée fairly coarsely.

3 Heat the oil in a frying pan, add the almond mixture and cook over low heat, stirring with a wooden spoon, for about 3–4 minutes. Scrape into the casserole or pan with the chicken.

4 Add water to the stock, if necessary, to make 2 cups. Stir it into the casserole or pan. Mix gently and simmer just long enough to blend the flavors and heat the chicken pieces through. Add salt to taste. Serve immediately, garnished with cilantro and accompanied by rice.

RICE PUDDING

R ice pudding is popular all over the world and is always different. This version – *arroz con leche* – is light and attractive and very easy to make.

INGREDIENTS
½ cup raisins
½ cup short-grain rice
1-inch strip of lime or lemon peel
1 cup water
2 cups milk
1 cup sugar
¼ teaspoon salt
1 inch cinnamon stick
2 egg yolks, well beaten
1 tablespoon unsalted
butter, cubed
toasted flaked almonds, to decorate
orange segments, to serve

SERVES 4

1 Put the raisins into a small bowl. Cover with warm water and set aside to soak. Put the short grain rice into a saucepan with the lime or lemon peel and water. Bring slowly to a boil and then lower the heat. Cover the pan and simmer very gently for about 20 minutes or until all the water has been absorbed.

2 Remove the peel from the rice and discard it. Add the milk, sugar, salt and cinnamon and cook, stirring, over very low heat, until all the milk has been absorbed. Do not cover the pan.

3 Discard the cinnamon stick. Add the egg yolks and cubed butter, stirring constantly until the butter has melted and the pudding is rich and creamy. Drain the raisins well and stir them into the rice. Cook the pudding for a few minutes longer.

4 Pour the rice into a dish and cool. Serve with the orange segments, decorated with the almonds.

COOK'S TIP
It is essential to use short-grain rice, which is sometimes called "pudding rice," for this pudding.

PUMPKIN IN BROWN SUGAR

his is a delicious way to make use of the abundance of pumpkin which is available at Halloween.

INGREDIENTS
1 pumpkin (2 pounds), cut into wedges
2 cups dark brown sugar
½ cup water
natural yogurt and brown sugar
(optional), to serve

SERVES 4

COOK'S TIP
The best pumpkin for this recipe is the classic orange-fleshed variety used to make jack o' lanterns. Choose one which will fit neatly into your casserole when cut.

1 Scrape the seeds out of the pumpkin wedges. Pack the wedges firmly together in a heavy flameproof casserole.

2 Divide the sugar among the pumpkin pieces, packing it into the hollows that contained the seeds.

3 Pour the water carefully into the casserole to cover the bottom and prevent the pumpkin from burning. Take care not to dislodge the sugar when pouring in the water.

4 Cover and cook over low heat, checking the water level frequently, until the pumpkin is tender and the sugar has dissolved in the liquid to form a sauce.

5 Using a slotted spoon, transfer the pumpkin to a serving dish. Pour the sugary liquid from the pan over the pumpkin and serve at once with plain yogurt, with a little brown sugar, if desired.

CHURROS

 eep fried strips of batter are served drenched in sugar for this delicious hot dessert.

INGREDIENTS
1 cup water
1 tablespoon sugar,
plus extra for dusting
½ teaspoon salt
1½ cups flour
1 large egg
oil, for frying
½ lime or lemon

MAKES ABOUT 24

COOK'S TIP
You can use a funnel to shape the *churros*. Close the end with a finger, add the batter, then release into the oil in small columns.

1 Bring the water, sugar and salt to a boil. Remove from the heat and beat in the flour until smooth.

2 Beat in the egg, using a wooden spoon, until the mixture is smooth and satiny. Set the batter aside.

3 Pour the oil into a deep frying pan to a depth of about 2 inches. Add the lime or lemon half, then heat the oil to 375°F or until a cube of day-old bread added to the oil browns in 30–60 seconds.

4 Pour the batter into a pastry bag fitted with a fluted nozzle. Pipe 3-inch strips of batter and then add to the oil, a few at a time. Fry for 3–4 minutes or until they are golden brown.

5 Using a slotted spoon, remove the *churros* from the pan and drain on paper towels. Roll the hot *churros* in granulated sugar before serving.

BUÑUELOS

his is one recipe out of many in Mexico which is based on a fried dough technique.

INGREDIENTS
2 cups flour
1 teaspoon baking powder
½ teaspoon salt
1 tablespoon sugar
1 large egg, beaten
½ cup milk
2 tablespoons unsalted butter, melted
oil, for frying
sugar, for dusting

FOR THE SYRUP
1⅓ cups light
brown sugar
3 cups water
1 inch cinnamon stick
1 clove

SERVES 6

1 Make the syrup first. Combine all the ingredients in a saucepan. Heat, stirring, until the sugar has dissolved, then leave to simmer until the mixture has reduced to a light syrup. Remove and discard the spices. Keep the syrup warm while you then make the *buñuelos*.

2 Sift the flour, baking powder and salt into a bowl. Stir in the sugar. In a mixing bowl, whisk the egg and the milk together. Gradually stir in the dry mixture, then beat in the melted butter to make a soft dough.

3 Turn the dough onto a lightly floured board and knead until it is smooth and elastic. Divide the dough into 18 pieces. Shape into balls. With your hands, flatten the balls into disk shapes about ¾ inch thick.

COOK'S TIP
Make the syrup ahead of time if you prefer, and chill it until you are ready to use it, when it can be warmed up quickly.

4 Use the floured handle of a wooden spoon to poke a hole through the center of each *buñuelo*. Pour oil into a deep frying pan to a depth of 2 inches. Alternatively, use a deep fryer. Heat the oil to 375°F or until a cube of day-old bread added to the oil browns in 30–60 seconds.

5 Fry the fritters in batches, taking care not to overcrowd the pan, until they are puffy and golden brown on both sides. Lift out with a slotted spoon and drain on paper towels. Dust the *buñuelos* with sugar and serve with the syrup.

COCONUT CUSTARD

his is another classic baked dessert. Adjust the amounts of cinnamon and coconut to taste.

INGREDIENTS
1 cup sugar
1 cup water
3 inch cinnamon stick
1 cup grated fresh coconut
3 cups milk
4 eggs
¾ cup whipping cream
3 tablespoons toasted chopped
almonds (optional)

SERVES 6

1 Combine the sugar, water and cinnamon stick in a large saucepan. Bring to a boil, then lower the heat and simmer, uncovered, for 5 minutes. Remove the cinnamon stick.

2 Add the grated coconut to the pan, and cook over low heat for 5 more minutes. Stir in the milk and cook, stirring occasionally, until the mixture has thickened to the consistency of thin custard. Remove from the heat and set aside.

3 Beat the eggs in a bowl until fluffy. Add a ladleful (3 tablespoons) of the coconut mixture to the eggs and stir well. Continue to add the coconut mixture in this way, then return the contents of the bowl to the clean pan. Stir well.

4 Cook over low heat, stirring constantly with a wooden spoon, until you have a thick custard. Pour into a serving dish.

5 Cool the custard, then chill until ready to serve. Whip the cream until thick and spread it over the custard. Decorate with toasted chopped almonds, if using.

COOK'S TIP
The easiest way to prepare a fresh coconut is to bake it in an oven preheated to 350°F for 15 minutes, then pierce two of the eyes with an ice pick or sharp skewer and drain out the milk. Open the coconut by hitting it carefully with a hammer; it will break into several pieces, making it easy to remove the shell. Peel off the brown skin, chop the flesh into small pieces and grate in a food processor.

SANGRIA

This very popular summer drink was borrowed from Spain. The Mexican version is slightly less alcoholic than the original.

INGREDIENTS

ice cubes
4 cups dry red table wine
⅔ cup freshly squeezed orange juice
¼ cup freshly squeezed lime juice
½ cup superfine sugar
2 limes or 1 apple, sliced, to serve

SERVES 6

COOK'S TIP

Sugar does not dissolve readily in alcohol. Use simple syrup, which is very easy to make and produces a smoother drink. Combine 2 cups water and 2 cups sugar in a bowl and set aside until the sugar has dissolved. Stir occasionally. One tablespoon of simple syrup is equal to 1½ teaspoons sugar.

1 Half fill a large pitcher with ice cubes. Pour in wine and orange and lime juices.

2 Add the sugar (or syrup, see Cook's Tip) and stir well until it has dissolved. Pour into tumblers and float the lime or apple slices on top. Serve immediately.

MARGARITA

Tequila is made from the sap of a fleshy-leafed plant called the blue agave and gets its name from the town of Tequila where it has been made for more than 200 years. The Margarita is the most popular and well-known drink made with tequila.

INGREDIENTS
½ lime or lemon
salt
½ cup white tequila
2 tablespoons Triple Sec or Cointreau
2 tablespoons freshly squeezed lime or lemon juice
4 or more ice cubes

SERVES 2

COOK'S TIP
It really is worth going to the trouble of buying limes for this recipe. Lemons will do, but the special flavor of the drink will be lost in the substitution.

1 Rub the rims of two cocktail glasses with the lime or lemon. Pour some salt into a saucer and dip the glasses in so the rims are frosted.

2 Combine the tequila, Triple Sec or Cointreau and lime or lemon juice in a pitcher and stir to mix well.

3 Pour the tequila mixture into the prepared glasses. Add the ice cubes and serve immediately.

ROSELLA DRINK

In Mexico, the bright red sepals of a tropical flowering plant, *Hibiscus sabdariffa*, are used to make drinks. Available fresh in the Caribbean at Christmas and dried here in the States, the plant is known in Mexico as *Flor de Jamaica* and elsewhere as *rosella* and *sorrel.* This drink is known as *Agua de Jamaica.*

INGREDIENTS
4 cups water
2 ounces rosella *sepals*
a little sugar

SERVES 4

2 Allow to boil gently, uncovered, for 1 minute, then remove from the heat and let stand for 15 minutes. Stir in a little sugar to sweeten. Strain into a pitcher. Cool, then cover and chill very well.

3 Serve the ice-cold rosella drink in long tumblers filled with ice.

1 Combine the water and *rosella* sepals in a large saucepan. Bring to a boil over medium heat.

COOK'S TIP
This soft drink can be made very festive with the addition of light rum. Mix 2 ounces light rum with an equal amount of Rosella Drink per serving.

CHOCOLATE CORN DRINK

I n Mexico, drinking chocolate is beaten with a very pretty carved wooden *molinillo*, but a wire whisk does the job just as well if not so decoratively. This traditional drink also contains *masa harina* and is known in Mexico as *champurrado*.

INGREDIENTS
½ cup masa harina
(tortilla flour)
3 cups water
2 inches cinnamon stick
3 cups milk
*3 squares Mexican chocolate,
or any unsweetened
chocolate, grated
a little light brown sugar*

SERVES 6

COOK'S TIP
If Mexican chocolate isn't available, use unsweetened chocolate instead.

1 Combine the *masa harina* and water in a large saucepan, stirring to mix well. Add the cinnamon stick and cook, stirring over low heat until the mixture thickens.

2 Gradually stir in the milk, then the grated chocolate. Continue to cook until all the chocolate has dissolved, beating with a whisk or a Mexican *molinillo*. Discard the cinnamon stick. Sweeten to taste with brown sugar. Serve hot in cups.

ROMPOPE

This drink could best be described as cooked eggnog. It keeps well if chilled but seldom lasts that long – it's so delicious it tends to vanish as if by magic! Serve as an aperitif.

INGREDIENTS
4 cups milk
1 cup sugar
2-inch cinnamon stick
½ cup ground almonds
12 large egg yolks
2 cups medium rum

MAKES ABOUT 7½ CUPS

COOK'S TIP
Try serving this over lots of ice in a tall tumbler for a deliciously long drink.

---

1 Combine the milk, sugar and cinnamon in a large saucepan. Simmer over very low heat, stirring constantly, until the sugar has dissolved.

2 Cool to room temperature. Remove the cinnamon stick and then stir in the ground almonds.

3 Beat the egg yolks in a bowl until they are very thick and pale.

4 Add the egg yolks to the almond mixture a little at a time, beating well. Return the pan to the heat and cook gently until the mixture coats a spoon. Cool.

5 Stir in the rum. Pour into a clean dry bottle and cork tightly. Keep in the fridge for 2 days before serving.

INDEX